ID0426598

refresh

These quotations were gathered lovingly but unscientifically over several years and/or contributed by many friends or acquaintances. Some arrived, and survived in our files, on scraps of paper and may therefore be imperfectly worded or attributed. To the authors, contributors and original sources, our thanks, and where appropriate, our apologies.—The editors

CREDITS

Compiled by Kobi Yamada
Designed by Steve Potter

ISBN: 1-888387-67-X

Printed in China

Give your soul some elbow room.

DENISE SHARP

A great time

to relax is when

you don't have

time for it.

SYDNEY HARRIS

FOR FAST-ACTING RELIEF TRY SLOWING DOWN.

LILY TOMLIN

Take time every day to do something ridiculous.

PHILIPA WALKER

My advice
in the midst of
the seriousness
is to keep
an eye out for
the tinker shuffle,
the flying of kites,
and kindred
sources of
surprised
amusement.

JEROME BRUNER

Live a balanced life.

Learn some and think some,

and draw and paint

and sing and dance

and play and work

every day some.

ROBERT FULGHUM

LEARN TO PAUSE...OR NOTHING
WORTHWHILE WILL CATCH UP TO YOU.

DOUG KING

Things to
do today:
Inhale,
exhale,
inhale,
exhale.
Ahhhh!

KOBI YAMADA

Several big ideas have come by taking a deep breath, leaving the building and taking a nice long walk in the sunshine down to get some ice cream.

NOLAN BUSHNELL

Hold out
your hands
to feel the
luxury of
the
sunbeams.

HELEN KELLER

Stress is basically a dis-
connection from the earth,
a forgetting of the breath...
My time was diced up into
minutes and hours rather
than into seasons and the
movement of the moon and
stars. Stress is a useless
state. It believes that everything is an emergency.

NATALIE GOLDBERG

There is
more to life than
simply increasing
its speed.

MAHATMA GANDHI

WE ALL
NEED TIME TO BE ALONE;
TO THINK, TO DREAM,
TO WONDER.

BILLIE ROARK

Rest is not a matter

of doing absolutely

nothing. Rest is repair.

DANIEL W. JOSSELYN

Always leave

enough room

in your life to

do something

that makes you

happy, satisfied,

or even joyous.

PAUL   HAWKEN

Our company prospered by cutting back to normal eight hour days, eliminating stressful reports, and simply talking to each other. Forty hours a week is plenty if you trust each other and have your priorities straight.

ROBERT MARCUS

The best
companies
will move
heaven and
earth
to help
their people
balance
their lives.

DAN ZADRA

TENSION IS WHO YOU THINK YOU SHOULD BE.
RELAXATION IS WHO YOU ARE.

CHINESE PROVERB

Within you
there is a stillness
and sanctuary
to which you
can retreat
at anytime and
be yourself.

HERMANN HESSE

Thoughts, rest your wings. Here is a hollow of silence, a nest of stillness, in which to hatch your dreams.

JOAN WALSH ANGLUND

Out of the daily chaos comes
the dance of balance.

DENISE KESTER

What is

this life if,

full of care,

we have no time

to stand and stare?

WILLIAM   HENRY   DAVIES

I LOAF AND INVITE MY SOUL.

WALT WHITMAN

When in doubt, take a bath.

MAE WEST

THERE MUST BE
QUITE A FEW THINGS A
HOT BATH
WON'T CURE, BUT
I DON'T KNOW
MANY OF THEM.

SYLVIA PLATH

I said in my heart,
'I am sick of four
walls and a ceiling.
I have a need of
the sky. I have
business with
the grass.'

RICHARD HOVEY

While you are upon the earth, enjoy the good things that are here.

JOHN SELDEN

Simple pleasures...

the last refuge

of the complex.

OSCAR WILDE

We are so distracted by our search for the extraordinary that we don't even recognize the sacred when we encounter it.

BARBARA DE ANGELIS, PH.D.

If you pay attention at every moment, you form a new relationship to time. In some magical way, by slowing down, you become more efficient, productive, and energetic, focusing without distraction directly on the task in front of you. Not only do you become immersed in the moment, you become that moment.

MICHAEL RAY

WHEN WE LOOK DEEP

INTO THE HEART OF

A FLOWER, WE SEE

CLOUDS, SUNSHINE,

MINERALS, TIME, THE

EARTH, AND EVERYTHING

ELSE IN THE COSMOS IN IT.

THICH NHAT HANH

Adopt the pace of nature.

RALPH WALDO EMERSON

Be where
you are;
otherwise
you will
miss
your life.

BUDDHA

TAKE TIME TO MARVEL AT THE
WONDERS OF LIFE.

GAIL LUNDY

The time
you enjoy
wasting
is not
wasted time.

BERTRAND RUSSELL

All the way

to heaven

is heaven.

ST. CATHERINE OF SIENA

These are the
magic years...
and therefore
magic days...
and therefore
magic moments.

ANONYMOUS

A good laugh is
sunshine in a house.

WILLIAM THACKERAY

If we're going to be able to look back

on something and laugh about it,

we might as well laugh about it now.

MARIE OSMOND

LAUGHTER IS AN INSTANT VACATION.

MILTON BERLE

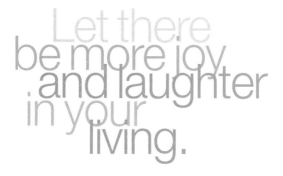

Let there
be more joy
and laughter
in your
living.

EILEEN CADDY

Those who wander
are not
necessarily lost.

KOBI YAMADA

It is good
to collect
things,
but it is
better
to go on
walks.

ANATOLE FRANCE

THE LESS OF ROUTINE,
THE MORE OF LIFE.

ALMOS B. ALCOTT

Balance
isn't
'either/or'
it's
'and.'

MARTIN SCULLY

YOU ONLY HAVE
ONE BODY—RESPECT IT.
YOU ONLY HAVE
ONE MIND—FEED IT.
YOU ONLY HAVE
ONE LIFE—LIVE AND
ENJOY IT.

DES'REE

Prevention is better than cure.

DESIDERIUS ERASMUS

Health is a state of complete physical, mental and social well-being, and not merely the absence of disease or infirmity.

HEAVE

I dance not

to get better

nor to fix myself,

I dance to remember

I am not sick.

MADELINE STERN

The essence of health

is an inner kind of balance.

ANDREW   WEIL,   M. D.

Every now and then go away and have a little relaxation. To remain constantly at work will diminish your judgment. Go some distance away, because work will be in perspective and a lack of harmony is more readily seen.

LEONARDO DA VINCI

Excess on occasion

is exhilarating; it

keeps moderation from

becoming a habit.

W. SOMERSET MAUGHM

Guard well your
spare moments. They are
like uncut diamonds.
Discard them and their
value will never be known.
Improve them and they
will become the brightest
gems in a useful life.

RALPH WALDO EMERSON

You will have wonderful surges forward. Then there must be a time of consolidating before the next forward surge. Accept this as part of the process and never become downhearted.

EILEEN CADDY

Muddy water,
    let stand,
becomes clear.

LAO-TZU

With beauty before me, may I walk. With beauty behind me, may I walk. With beauty above me, may I walk. With beauty below me, may I walk. With beauty all around me, may I walk. Wandering on a trail of beauty, lively, may I walk.

NAVAJO PRAYER

Balance is beautiful.

MIYOKI OHNO

the good life™

Celebrating the joy of living fully.

Also available from Compendium Publishing are these spirited companion books in The Good Life series of great quotations:

yes!

moxie

hero

friend

heart

spirit

success

joy

thanks

These books may be ordered directly
from the publisher (800) 914-3327.
But please try your local bookstore first!

www.compendiuminc.com